The **Essential** Buyer's Guide

New
MINI

All models 2001 to 2006

T0150288

Your marque expert:
Martyn Collins

VELOCE PUBLISHING
THE PUBLISHER OF FINE AUTOMOTIVE BOOKS

Also from Veloce Publishing –

Essential Buyer's Guide Series

Alfa GT (Booker)
Alfa Romeo Spider Giulia (Booker & Talbott)
Austin Seven (Barker)
Big Healeys (Trummel)
BMW E21 3 Series (1975-1983) (Reverente, Cook)
BMW GS (Henshaw)
BSA Bantam (Henshaw)
BSA 500 & 650 Twins (Henshaw)
Citroën 2CV (Paxton)
Citroën ID & DS (Heilig)
Cobra Replicas (Ayre)
Corvette C2 Sting Ray 1963-1967 (Falconer)
Ducati Bevel Twins (Falloon)
Fiat 500 & 600 (Bobbitt)
Ford Capri (Paxton)
Harley-Davidson Big Twins (Henshaw)
Hinckley Triumph triples & fours 750, 900, 955, 1000, 1050, 1200 – 1991-2009 (Henshaw)
Honda CBR600 Hurricane (Henshaw)
Honda CBR FireBlade (Henshaw)
Honda SOHC fours 1969-1984 (Henshaw)
Jaguar E-type 3.8 & 4.2-litre (Crespin)
Jaguar E-type V12 5.3-litre (Crespin)
Jaguar XJ 1995-2003 (Crespin)
Jaguar XK8 & XKR (1996-2005) (Thorley)
Jaguar/Daimler XJ6, XJ12 & Sovereign (Crespin)
Jaguar/Daimler XJ40 (Crespin)
Jaguar Mark 1 & 2 (All models including Daimler 2.5-litre V8) 1955 to 1969 (Thorley)
Jaguar XJ-S (Crespin)
Jaguar XK 120, 140 & 150 (Thorley)
Land Rover Series I, II & IIA (Thurman)
Mazda MX-5 Miata (Mk1 1989-97 & Mk2 98-2001) (Crook)
Mercedes-Benz 280SL-560DSL Roadsters (Bass)
Mercedes-Benz 'Pagoda' 230SL, 250SL & 280SL Roadsters & Coupés (Bass)
MGA 1955-1962 (Sear, Crosier)
MGB & MGB GT (Williams)
MG Midget & A-H Sprite (Horler)
MG TD, TF & TF1500 (Jones)
Mini (Paxton)
Morris Minor & 1000 (Newell)
New MINI (Collins)
Norton Commando (Henshaw)
Peugeot 205 GTI (Blackburn)
Porsche 911 (930) Turbo series (Streather)
Porsche 911 (964) (Streather)
Porsche 911 (993) (Streather)
Porsche 911 (996) (Streather)
Porsche 911 Carrera 3.2 series 1984 to 1989 (Streather)
Porsche 911SC – Coupé, Targa, Cabriolet & RS Model years 1978-1983 (Streather)
Porsche 924 – All models 1976 to 1988 (Hodgkins)
Porsche 928 (Hemmings)
Porsche 986 Boxster series (Streather)
Porsche 987 Boxster and Cayman series (Streather)
Rolls-Royce Silver Shadow & Bentley T-Series (Bobbitt)
Subaru Impreza (Hobbs)
Triumph Bonneville (Henshaw)
Triumph Herald & Vitesse (Davies, Mace)

Triumph Spitfire & GT6 (Baugues)
Triumph Stag (Mort & Fox)
Triumph TR6 (Williams)
Triumph TR7 & TR8 (Williams)
Vespa Scooters – Classic 2-stroke models 1960-2008 (Paxton)
VW Beetle (Cservenka & Copping)
VW Bus (Cservenka & Copping)
VW Golf GTI (Cservenka & Copping)

From Veloce Publishing's new imprints:

BATTLE CRY!

Soviet General & field rank officer uniforms: 1955 to 1991 (Streather)
Red & Soviet military & paramilitary services: female uniforms 1941-1991 (Streather)

Hubble & Hattie

The Grooming Bible – The definitive guide to the science, practice and art of dog grooming for students and home groomers (Gould & Ferguson)
A dog's dinner – Practical, healthy and nutritious recipes for REAL dog food (Paton-Ayre)
Animal Grief – How animals mourn (Alderton)
Cat Speak – recognising and understanding behaviour (Rauth-Widmann)
Clever Dog! – life lessons from the world's most successful animal (O'Meara)
Complete Dog Massage Manual, The – Gentle Dog Care (Robertson)
Dieting with my dog – one busy life, two full figures ... and unconditional love (Frezon)
Dinner with Rover – Delicious, nutritious meals for you and your dog to share (Paton-Ayre)
Dog Relax – Relaxed dogs, relaxed owners (Pilguj)
Dog Speak – recognising and understanding behaviour (Blenski)
Emergency first aid for dogs – Home and away (Bucksch)
Exercising your puppy: a gentle & natural approach – Gentle Dog Care (Robertson)
Fun and games for cats! (Seidl)
Know Your Dog – The guide to a beautiful relationship (Birmelin)
Life skills for puppies – Laying the foundation for a loving, lasting relationship (Mills & Zulch)
Living with an Older Dog – Gentle Dog Care (Alderton & Hall)
Miaow! Cats really are nicer than people! (Moore)
My dog has arthritis ... but lives life to the full! (Carrick)
My dog has cruciate ligament injury – but lives life to the full! (Häusler)
My dog has hip dysplasia – but lives life to the full! (Häusler)
My dog is blind – but lives life to the full! (Horsky)
My dog is deaf – but lives life to the full! (Willms)
Partners – Everyday working dogs being heros every day (Walton)
Smellorama – nose games for dogs (Theby)
Swim to recovery: Canine hydrotherapy healing (Wong)
The truth about wolves and dogs – Dispelling the myths of dog training (Shelbourne)
Waggy Tails & Wheelchairs (Epp)
Walking the dog – motorway walks for drivers and dogs (Rees)
Walking the dog in France – motorway walks for drivers and dogs (Rees)
Winston ... the dog who changed my life (Klute)
You and Your Border Terrier – The Essential Guide (Alderton)
You and Your Cockapoo – The Essential Guide (Alderton)

www.veloce.co.uk

First published in June 2012 by Veloce Publishing Limited, Veloce House, Parkway Farm Business Park, Middle Farm Way, Poundbury, Dorchester, Dorset, DT1 3AR, England.
Fax 01305 250479/e-mail info@veloce.co.uk/web www.veloce.co.uk or www.velocebooks.com.

ISBN: 978-1-845844-08-0 UPC: 6-36847-04408-4

Introduction
– the purpose of this book

How do you replace a motoring icon? It took 42 years and a change of ownership, but on July 7 2001, the first UK MINI dealers opened for business, and lucky owners took delivery of their Ones and Coopers. The MINI's mixture of cheeky styling, quality build, sharp handling and low running costs, along with the TLC servicing package, caught the eye of buyers worldwide, and it wasn't long before the new car was accepted in a similar way to the Issigonis original, becoming a modern icon.

Spin forward to the present. The first MINIs are now over ten years old and outside the dealer chain. This book is designed to assist with the buying process, from the earliest R50 cars right through to the first of the second generation R56 models.

Believe it or not, BMW was actually worried as to whether it was going to make any money out of the MINI brand, so it was a bit of surprise when it decided to keep it, after the Rover sell off in March 2000. After all, BMW had no experience in producing a premium small car. Still, it shouldn't have worried, as even with a laboured development process between the UK and Germany, the end result was loved by the press and public alike.

Recreating motoring icons was nothing new in the noughties. Before the MINI arrived, the Volkswagen Beetle had been launched, but unlike the re-bodied Golf, the MINI really seemed to capture the imagination of buyers wanting their own unique premium small car. This was where the MINI scored an own goal, though, as the vast array of colours, trims and option packs meant that no two cars that came out of the Oxford factory were ever the same.

If there was one criticism besides the poor interior space, it was the Cooper's relative lack of puff. This was

The first view of the modern MINI, the 1996 Paris Motor Show concept. (Courtesy MINI UK)

Almost production-ready, but check out the badging and twin exhausts! (Courtesy MINI UK)

Roger 'The Hat' Wall's Chili Red Cooper; the first New MINI ordered.

solved by the fitment of a Roots supercharger, and the introduction of the Cooper S a year later in July 2002. The MINI is still considered to be one of the most complete hot hatches ever, and has attracted the attention of enthusiasts and tuners alike.

There are plenty of MINIs available in hatchback and convertible body styles, from the entry-level One, through to the warm Cooper, and at the top of the MINI performance tree, the Cooper S. With such a massive choice of models, there's a MINI to suit most budgets, and using the unique points system in this guide will help you find a great car at the right price.

Much of what is covered in this book is about original equipment manufacturer versions (OEM) but there are a small number of special edition versions, such as the John Cooper Works (JCW) GP, which has a certain cachet amongst enthusiasts, and this is reflected in the higher than average prices.

Thanks

I've been lucky enough to own BMW MINIs since 2002, and I've driven most models in the range during my many motoring journalism roles. I've gradually worked my way up from a One, through to a Cooper, then on to the second generation Cooper and Cooper Clubman version. Then, in 2010, despite a heavily pregnant wife, I got the chance to own my dream MINI, the ultra-rare Cooper S, JCW GP.

My ownership experience has been enhanced by membership of forums, where friendship and advice has always been available. In the early days it was MINI2.com, then latterly totalMINI.com and the GP UK owners' club. I'd like to thank all of the members who I have come into contact with over the last ten years; they have given me support and pointed me in the right direction when needed.

Thanks must also go to Sarah Heaney and Jemma Chalcroft at MINI UK, Roger 'The Hat' Wall of the Herts and North London Mini Cooper Register, Andrey Magiy and Emma Dutton at Lohen, and Chris Porter and Paul Travers at Specialist Cars Stevenage.

Contents

The Essential Buyer's Guide™ currency
At the time of publication a BG unit of currency "●" equals approximately
£1.00/US$1.58/Euro 1.19. Please adjust to suit current exchange rates.

1 Is it the right car for you?
– marriage guidance

Tall and short drivers
Considering how much bigger the New MINI is over the '60s original, the interior is either a massive hit or big failure, depending on where you sit. The MINI is blessed with a fine driving position, with both the seats and steering column being multi-adjustable.

Weight of controls
The electric power-assisted steering is light and full of feel, only weighting up at low speeds. Both the clutch and brake pedals have a delicate and progressive feel.

Will it fit in the garage?
The MINI might have ballooned in length to 3.63 metres (11.89ft), but it should still be small enough to fit in most garages. All-round visibility is generally good, but Park Distance Control (PDC) was available as an option.

Interior space
Space in the front of a MINI is sadly at the expense of rear legroom, but it can comfortably accomodate two adults and two children. Headroom is good and the windows are big enough so it doesn't feel too claustrophobic in the back.

Luggage capacity
If you need to carry big loads then a MINI isn't really for you, as to be frank, like the rear legroom, boot space is poor (160 litres). Still, the two rear seats fold independently to give more room, and the hatch makes access easy.

Running costs
Two years or 10,000 miles recommended oil service intervals, but full service intervals are every 20,000 miles. Fuel economy is good, but not amazing. The MINI One D is best with its almost 60mpg fuel figure.

Usability
A great all-rounder, the MINI is equally at home in town and on country roads.

Parts availability
There should be no problems getting parts and if BMW/MINI can't help, there's an established network of specialists that should be able to. Some JCW parts, however, are getting harder to get hold of.

Parts cost
Service and parts prices are generally reasonable; however some specialist parts will be more expensive.

Insurance
The One and Cooper have the lowest insurance group. The Cooper S is higher, starting at group 15, but this hike is in line with the extra performance.

Not really a four-seater: space in the rear of a MINI is tight.

Investment potential
All models are depreciating, but special edition models such as the GP are doing better than the rest of the range and are most likely to retain value longer.

Plus points
The BMW MINI looks great, is fun to drive and is relatively cost effective to own.

Minus points
There's virtually no rear legroom or boot space. First generation Cooper S models are thirsty with higher running costs.

Alternatives
Ford Puma, Volkswagen Beetle.

2 Cost considerations
– affordable, or a money pit?

In general, running costs are reasonable but can be high for more powerful models, especially the Cooper S, as you'll pay more for insurance and fuel.

Service periods
Oil service: every 10-12,000 miles
Inspection I service: every 25,000 miles
Inspection II service: 50,000 miles
Convertible roof/hood: ●x1450
Inspection I service (dealer): ●x159
Inspection II service (dealer): ●x249
Small service (specialist): ●x155
Large service (specialist): ●x215
Used engine (specialist): from ●x450
Reconditioned gearbox (5-speed): ●x400
Brake caliper (front): ●x147.50

Brake caliper (rear): ●x154
Brake disc: ●x55
Brake pads: ●x49.74
Brake pad sensor*: ●x13.75
Wheel bearing (front): ●x144.17
Wheel bearing (rear): ●x150
Bonnet (standard): ●x300
Front bumper (standard): ●x216
Front bumper (Cooper S): ●x195
Front strut: ●x86
Steering rack: ●x725
*Has to be changed at the same time as the brake pads.

Parts that are hard to find
BMW has a history of producing masses of parts for its cars and keeping them on the shelves. However, if you're after specialist JCW bits, parts supplies are dwindling – especially items of trim. For that elusive part, online auctions are probably your best bet.

The Cooper S's supercharged engine offers the best performance, but you will pay at the pumps and with insurance.

Cooper front bumper with chrome inserts, part of the Chili pack.

3 Living with a MINI
– will you get along together?

Good points

If you're looking for a well-built small car with unique looks and heritage, then the MINI could be for you. Just looking at BMW's re-working of the Classic Mini shape is sure to put a smile on your face, and considering you're buying one of the best front-wheel drive cars ever, good value too.

The entry-level R50 One is entertaining to drive, with crisp steering and nifty handling – you'll be amazed at how quickly you can go round corners! The Cooper, Cooper S and John Cooper Works (JCW, the factory performance brand for the MINI) badges, link with fast Minis of the past. The fact that these cars are so tuneable, and can handle big power means that they still have a following amongst hot hatch fans, despite the newer, more powerful rivals that are now on the scene.

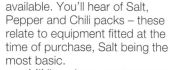

The entry-level MINI is the One, with a 90bhp version of the 1.6-litre engine. (Courtesy MINI UK)

It's not just speed where the BMW MINI impresses; for a small car, the standard ride is supple, its clutch, light and the 5- and 6-speed manual gearboxes have a precise change. This makes for easy in-town driving, but get out of the city and generally the MINI is a relaxed cruiser, feeling planted at speed. The Cooper's reputation for its: "sports car performance and handling wrapped in a cute design that's practical and affordable," was recognised in 2003, when this model won the highly respected North American Car of the Year title.

Another plus point is the wide selection of colours, trims and options that were available. You'll hear of Salt, Pepper and Chili packs – these relate to equipment fitted at the time of purchase, Salt being the most basic.

MINI engines are strong as long as they are looked after. Servicing and parts costs, even at dealers, are reasonable. All MINIs came with a three-year 60,000 mile warranty and six years anti-corrosion. Finally,

There's plenty of space in the front and the driving position is excellent in a MINI.

Owning a MINI can be a social experience, as this gathering of GPs shows.

like the Issigonis original, the MINI has a large following of enthusiasts who make up an active online community, keen to welcome new members, and offering advice and information to owners, plus an extensive knowledge of all things MINI.

The owners' club experience is supported by a large network of official and independent dealers and specialists that can help keep the car on the road, or can help you make modifications, with a vast choice of interior, exterior or engine options.

Bad points

The MINI might be great to look at, sit in and drive, but there's no getting away from the poor interior space. There isn't enough room for adult passengers to sit comfortably in the back on long trips, and the boot is tiny.

The R53 Cooper S is thirsty, especially if you use all the performance. Drive it hard and expect consumption to fall below 20mpg; this can drop to just over 15mpg if you enjoy track work.

Road noise on cars fitted with 17in or 18in alloy wheels and sports suspension can be hard work on long motorway trips.

First generation MINIs are generally well-built, and quality improved throughout their production life, but the attractive interior is prone to trim and dashboard rattles.

Boot space is not a MINI strong point; still, the two rear seats fold to increase practicality.

Standard R50 and R53 Cooper and Cooper S models fitted with the JCW tuning pack are serious performers. With this power comes a responsibility to keep within speed limits, and penalty points are a real possibility.

Finally, despite the close relationship with the original, there are still plenty of Classic Mini owners who refuse to accept this car. This can make attending some social events difficult.

4 Models compared
– which is the one for you?

For your guidance, this chapter aims to give you an idea of the differences between the various New MINI models.

Regardless of model, cars in excellent condition, with desirable options, good service history and low mileage are what you should be looking for.

First generation

R50 MINI One
The entry-level MINI is ideal for fuel efficiency (41.5mpg), or for young or new drivers, due to its group 5 insurance. Mechanically the same as the quicker Cooper, you'll need to work the 90bhp 1.6-litre engine hard to get the best out of it.

R50 MINI One D
Want a fun-to-drive package with almost 60mpg economy? The One D could be the MINI for you. Powered by a 75bhp, 1.4-litre Toyota-diesel engine, performance is modest at best. With the lightweight engine, the One D retains the MINI's go-kart feel.

R52 MINI One Convertible
The One is the cheapest way into a MINI Convertible, and ideal if you want the drop-top looks with 41.5mpg fuel economy and reasonable group 6 insurance. Heavier than the MINI hatch due to the lack of roof (and thus a reinforced body), the handling isn't as sharp.

If you value diesel economy over performance, the R50 MINI One D could be the car for you. (Courtesy MINI UK)

R50 MINI One Seven
First of a trio of heritage-inspired limited editions introduced in 2005. Available in exclusive Solar Red metallic, Astro Black, Pepper White and Pure Silver paint finishes; special features include 'Seven' cloth interior trim, 15in Delta alloy wheels and 'Seven' decals/stickers. Standard equipment was enhanced with manual air-conditioning and an onboard computer.

R50 MINI Cooper
The Cooper has more performance, but should still prove cost-effective to run with group 8 insurance and fuel economy of 40.9mpg. This warmer MINI also has the cachet of that historic name, extra chrome and sportier looks.

R50 MINI Cooper with John Cooper Works conversion
A Cooper fitted with the JCW factory-approved performance kit offered as a dealer fit option. The

R50 Cooper is the warm model in the MINI range, with 115bhp and a 9.2 second 0-62 time.

kit includes a performance cylinder head, ECU re-map, sports exhaust and air filter. Modifications were similar to JCW UK Challenge racers and performance gains were modest.

R52 MINI Cooper Convertible
Essentially the same as the One convertible, the Cooper has slightly more power, chrome and equipment.

R50 MINI Cooper Park Lane
Another of the heritage-inspired limited edition MINIs launched in 2005. Finished in exclusive Royal Grey metallic paint, with silver roof and mirror caps, other special features included 'Park Lane' leather trim, 16in Bridge Spoke alloy wheels, Park Lane decals, special silver bonnet stripes, and a three-spoke steering wheel.

R53 MINI Cooper S
The S is powered by the same 1.6-litre engine, but gains a supercharger and intercooler, giving extra oomph with power up to 163bhp or 170bhp (if you go for a face-lifted model from 2004 onwards). It also has a 6-speed gearbox and sports suspension, but it's more expensive to run as it's thirsty and costs more to insure and tax.

The MINI Cooper Park Lane was released in 2006, and is one of a trio of heritage limited editions released towards the end of the first generation R50 production.

R53 MINI Cooper S with John Cooper works conversion
A Cooper S fitted with the JCW factory-approved performance kit offered originally as a dealer-fit option. The kit includes an uprated supercharger and cylinder head, ECU re-map, sports exhaust and air filter. The result was up to 210bhp and a giant-killing top speed of 143mph.

R52 MINI Cooper S Convertible
The quickest MINI Convertible has the same 170bhp, but is thirstier than the hatch, and subject to high tax and insurance premiums.

R50 MINI Cooper S Checkmate
Another of the heritage-inspired limited edition MINIs launched in 2005. Only available with Space Blue metallic paint, special features include 'Checkmate' cloth and leather trim, 17in flame-spoke alloy wheels and 'Checkmate' decals. Added standard

R52 Cooper S Convertible is the quickest drop-top MINI.

equipment included a limited-slip differential and xenon headlights.

R53 Cooper S GP 2006
Possibly the ultimate R53 Cooper S, just 2000 GPs were produced by Bertone in Italy just before R56 production began in 2006. The GP is fitted with a unique bodykit, 18in alloy wheels and Thunder blue metallic paint finish. Just a two-seater, the GP's exclusivity is assured with only 455 individually numbered cars sold in the UK.

R53 MINI Cooper S MC40 2004
A USA-only special edition, celebrating the 40th anniversary of winning the 1964 Monte Carlo rally. Just 1000 of these Chili red and white MINI Cooper S versions were available, with features including unique graphics, anthracite R90 17in alloy wheels, driving lamps, chromed grille and mirror caps. Inside, there's unique red and black leather trim, a carbon-fibre dashboard, and a numbered plaque on the centre console.

Second generation
R56 MINI Cooper
It might look the same, but the R56 second generation car is very different underneath to the R53. Gone is the Chrysler Tritec engine, replaced by a more efficient and sophisticated, 120bhp, 1.6-litre Peugeot/Citroën-supplied engine mated with 6-speed manual transmission. Inside, there's a higher quality interior.

R56 MINI Cooper S
It might still have the bonnet scoop, but like the Cooper, the S is significantly changed underneath. Gone is the charismatic supercharged engine, replaced by a punchy and surprisingly frugal turbocharged, 175bhp version of the 1.6-litre Peugeot/Citroën-supplied engine. Inside is the same high quality interior.

With the John Cooper Works parts and exclusive body styling, the GP is one of the most revered amongst MINI limited editions.

MINI deliberately didn't mess too much with the exterior styling of the second generation R56 MINI, as this 2006 Cooper shows.

The second generation R56 MINI Cooper S, introduced to all markets, was turbocharged rather than supercharged. (Courtesy MINI UK)

5 Before you view
– be well informed

To avoid a wasted journey, and the disappointment of finding that the car does not match your expectations, it helps to be clear about what questions you want to ask before you pick up the telephone. Some of these points might appear basic, but when you're excited about the prospect of buying your dream MINI, it's amazing how some of the most obvious things slip the mind. Check the current values of the model you wish to view; these can be found in car magazines and dedicated price guides.

Where is the car?
Is it going to be worth travelling to the next county/state, or even across a border? A locally advertised car, although it may not sound very interesting, could be worth a visit and add to your knowledge – it might even be in better condition than expected.

Dealer or private sale?
Establish early on if the car is being sold by its owner or by a trader. A private owner should have all the history. A dealer may have more limited knowledge, but should have some documentation. A dealer may offer a warranty/guarantee (ask for a printed copy) and finance.

Cost of collection and delivery
A dealer may well be used to quoting for delivery by car transporter. A private owner may agree to meet you halfway, but only agree to this after you have seen the car at the vendor's address to validate the documents. You could meet halfway and agree the sale, but insist on meeting at the vendor's address for the handover.

View – when and where?
It is always preferable to view at the vendor's home or business premises. In the case of a private sale, the car's documentation should tally with the vendor's name and address. Arrange to view only in daylight, and avoid a wet day. Most cars look better in poor light or when wet.

Reason for sale?
Make it one of your first questions. Why is the car being sold, and how long has it been with the current owner? How many previous owners?

Service history?
Does the car have a full service history (preferably by MINI dealerships or specialists)?

Modified?
Cars that have been modified must be given special attention, and have written documentation to support the quality of the work carried out.

Condition (body/chassis/interior/mechanicals)?
Ask for an honest appraisal of the car's condition. Ask specifically about some of the check items described in chapter 7.

All original specification?
An original equipment car is invariably of higher value than a customised version.

Matching data/legal ownership?
Do VIN/chassis, engine numbers and licence plate match the official registration document? Is the owner's name and address recorded in the official registration documents?

For those countries requiring an annual test of roadworthiness, does the car have a document showing it complies? (An MoT certificate in the UK, which can be verified on 0845 600 5977).

If a smog/emissions certificate is mandatory, does the car have one?

If required, does the car carry a current road fund licence/licence plate tag?

Does the vendor own the car outright? Money might be owed to a finance company or bank; the car could even be stolen. Several organisations will supply the data on ownership, based on the car's licence plate number, for a fee. Such companies can often also tell you whether the car has been 'written-off' by an insurance company. In the UK these organisations can supply vehicle data:

HPI   tel 01722 422 422
AA   tel 0870 600 0836
DVLA   tel 0300 790 6802
RAC   tel 0870 533 3660

Other countries have similar organisations.

Insurance
Check with your existing insurer before setting out. Your current policy might not cover you to drive the car if you do purchase it.

How you can pay?
A cheque (check) will take several days to clear, and the seller may prefer a cash buyer. However, a banker's draft (a cheque issued by a bank) is as good as cash, but safer. Your bank will tell you how to obtain a banker's draft.

Buying at auction
If the intention is to buy at auction see chapter 10 for further advice.

Professional vehicle check (mechanical examination)
There are often marque/model specialists who will undertake a professional examination of a vehicle on your behalf. Owners' clubs can put you in touch with such specialists.

Other organisations that will carry out a general professional check in the UK are:

AA   www.theaa.com tel 0800 085 3007 (UK motoring organisation with vehicle inspectors)
RAC   www.rac.co.uk tel 0870 533 3660 (UK motoring organisation with vehicle inspectors)
AAA   www.aaa.com (US motoring organisation with vehicle inspection centres)

Other countries have similar organisations.

6 Inspection equipment
– these items will really help

Before you rush out of the door, gather together a few items to help as you work your way around the car.

This book
This book is designed to be your guide at every step, so take it along and use the check boxes to help you assess each area of the car you're interested in. Don't be afraid to let the seller see you using it.

Glasses (spectacles)
Take your reading glasses if you need them to read documents and make close-up inspections.

Magnet
A magnet will help you check if the car is full of filler (Bondo). Use the magnet to sample bodywork areas all around the car, but be careful not to damage the paintwork.

Torch
A torch with fresh batteries will be useful for peering into the wheel arches and under the car.

Probe or small screwdriver
A small screwdriver can be used – with care – as a probe, particularly in the wheelarches and on the underside.

Overalls
Be prepared to get dirty. Take along a pair of overalls, if you have them.

Mirror on a stick
Fixing a mirror at an angle on the end of a stick may seem odd, but you'll probably need it to check the condition of the underside of the car. It will also help you to peer into some of the important crevices. You can also use it, together with the torch, along the underside of the sills (rockers) and floor.

Digital camera
If you have the use of a digital camera, take it along so that, later, you can study some areas of the car more closely. Take a picture of any part of the car that causes you concern, and seek a friend's opinion.

Ideally, have a friend or knowledgeable enthusiast accompany you; a second opinion is always valuable.

7 Fifteen minute evaluation
– walk away or stay?

Exterior

With interest in the BMW MINI from owners and enthusiasts alike, and over 130,000 sold in the UK alone, there should be plenty of choice, and a good chance of finding a well-maintained car.

Built to BMW standards, the quality improved consistently from launch onwards. But a car is only as good as its owner, so be on the look out for damage. The first thing to check is the paintwork – is the finish the same on all the panels? Any inconsistencies could indicate repairs, fresh paint, or most likely both. Is there any evidence in the paperwork? The MINI has quite upright front styling so expect stonechips – especially on early cars. If there aren't, ask why, as there might be more serious repairs disguised.

Stonechips are common on the leading edge of the bonnet; other damage will need closer investigation.

Next, consider the overall condition of the bodywork. Look for small parking dents on the doors and rear quarters, scratches, poor panel fit (especially the bonnet and bumpers), evidence of overspray and marks under the paintwork. If the car you're looking at has obvious signs of repair and no explanation is given – walk away – it could have been poorly repaired after a serious accident.

The limited edition GP was fitted with a unique bodykit, so make sure it's all still fitted to the car and in good condition; replacement parts such as the rear wing are costly. With such a booming trade in official and unofficial accessories, body modifications are common; aero side skirts, front and rear bumpers and bigger rear spoilers are popular. Make sure they've been correctly fitted.

If you're looking at a convertible, check the condition of the hood. Is the material free of wear and tears? If there's damage this could prove expensive to repair.

Take a look at the underside, paying particular attention to the bottom of the front bumper, which is quite low and easily caught on high kerbs when parking. Anything other than superficial scratching could have been caused by careless driving. If you're not happy with your first inspection, further checks might be needed to see if any damage is serious.

MINIs are available with a vast choice of official and aftermarket alloy wheels, in 15in, 16in, 17in and 18in sizes. Don't be surprised to find that owners might have upgraded to bigger rims, even if the MINI drives better and was developed on the smallest wheels. Examine each wheel for

Query the cause of damage to the car, such as that shown here on the bumper.

Inspect alloy wheels for kerbing or scratching; serious damage can be costly.

Spotlights are a popular accessory; check their condition carefully as they are prone to damage.

signs of kerbing or scratching. Expect some damage, but be aware that repairs can be costly, especially those with the optional white finish. As the MINI is front-wheel drive, it's the front tyres that take the most punishment. You'll be lucky to get 15,000 miles out of a set of front tyres, particularly if the car is driven hard. This is especially true of high powered Cooper S models. Rear tyres wear out less quickly than front ones. Are all the tyres the same make and rating? Does the seller have records of how often they have been changed? If the tyres are wearing unevenly and the wheels are damaged this could indicate that they are out of alignment. This will affect the MINI's handling and a pricey alignment check is the only way of knowing if there's a problem.

Only JCW models have a unique conversion plaque on the top of the engine.

Front spots and different rear lights are inexpensive and popular modifications. If the front spots are official MINI accessories, check for signs of corrosion and pitting in the chrome finish. The early designed chromed lights don't stand up well to road salt and unless they're looked after, they will rust. Replacements are costly. Always check the wiring carefully if there have been any electrical upgrades.

Roof graphics are a popular option or aftermarket modification on MINIs; check they're not peeling or faded. Wing mirror covers are another common modification and are easy to add or remove.

Make sure both metal MINI badges are present front and back. Check that the car you're looking at is actually what it claims to be. Many of the badges can be bought from aftermarket suppliers and online auctions. Remember, it's very easy to make a One look like a Cooper. JCW semi-circular badges were only fitted to cars with the tuning kits. Check for an engine-mounted conversion plaque with its unique number.

Interior

If the car you're looking at has standard front seats make sure they're not saggy, with split fabric. Front seats on early cars were subject to a recall because they locked in the folded position; check they fold and slide correctly. Look at the plastic backs of the front seats, as they are prone to scratching. Expect some damage, but if there's too much, questions should be asked as to how the car has been used.

Supportive Recaro seats are standard in a GP, but were a costly option on the Cooper and Cooper S.

Feel the carpet in the front footwells of early cars; dampness could indicate a water leak from the A-pillar. This is quite serious, as the ECU and one of the body control modules on R53 models live here. If water has been getting in for a while, expect a range of electrical faults.

The biggest change to the interior was the 2004 re-fresh; these models feature a revised dash, less prone to rattles, with the passenger airbag moved to the dash top. It was at this time that more interior options were offered for personalisation. These included a sport chrono pack, where the centre speedo was replaced by larger versions of the fuel and temperature gauges, with the rev-counter and speedo moving to the steering column. Sat nav, a chrome interior pack, colour-coded dashboard and door panels were also available.

A Boost CD stereo was offered on all R50 generation MINIs.

Two of the key selling points of the first generation limited edition models (the Cooper Park Lane, Cooper S Checkmate and the Cooper S GP), were the special interior trim and the GP's standard Recaro sports seats (although they were a costly option on the Checkmate and standard Cooper S models). These models in good condition are always worth a look because of their rarity and are worth the extra cash if the condition of the rest of the car stacks up.

The standard BMW stereos are easily replaced, so don't be too surprised if you find an aftermarket unit. Later R56 models, however, have the stereo built into the dashboard.

Expect different steering wheels, gear knobs, pedals, and extra gauges on the dash. These parts often improve the interior, but if they've been fitted by the owner make sure they've been correctly installed.

Mechanicals

The earliest MINIs are over ten years old, so don't expect the engine bay to be pristine. However, questions should be asked if it's a dirty, oily mess.

A key thing to check on first generation MINIs, is the oil-filled circular engine mount on the right-hand side of the engine. A known weak point, look for black oily deposits on the chassis leg, as this could indicate a failing engine mount. A test

The front-mounted radiator is vulnerable to damage from stones; check for leaks and damage to the slats.

drive should confirm this, as there will be stronger vibrations from the engine. Budget approximately ●x200 for an engine mount replacement at a dealer.

Now, pull the dipstick and check there's plenty of oil, and that the condition corresponds with the mileage. The MINI has long servicing intervals, but if the oil is black and smells burnt, a service is going to be due very soon, so factor this cost into any offer price.

Next, look at the condition of the small, front-mounted radiator. If the car is fitted with air-conditioning, there will be a smaller radiator-like condenser on top. There's not a lot to see, but look for signs of leaks and stains around the edges. Check the overall condition of the slats; are there any that have been bent? Due to the design of the MINI's nose, radiators are prone to damage from stones and other road debris coming through the upper and lower grilles.

At the back of the engine, check the condition of the plastic brake fluid reservoir. MINI refined the design over the course of R53 production because of failures due to leaks or cracking. Look for staining on the bulkhead, back of the engine, and on the reservoir itself.

Complete your evaluation of the engine by getting the seller to start it; listen for any unusual knocks and rattles. If it's a Cooper or Cooper S and there's a slight rattle at the top end, this could either indicate a problem with the hydraulic tappets, or that the timing chain needs tensioning. Slowly bring the revs up and listen for a bottom-end rattle. If you can hear one, it's likely that the car you're looking at has run low on oil at some stage, and now has excessive bearing clearances.

Does the engine look or sound standard? Cone-type air-filters and sports exhausts are common modifications. If the exhaust has been modified, make sure you and your neighbours can live with the noise. Remember that any modifications could affect your insurance if they are not declared.

Finally, if the car you're viewing is fitted with air-conditioning, make sure you test it's working by going from hot to cold settings – cold air should come quickly!

Documents
A full official MINI dealer service history is best, but don't be surprised if older cars have a mix of official and specialist stamps. Check the service book and any receipts to make sure that regular servicing has been maintained. The car's identification number (VIN) is stamped on a sticker located on the right-hand side of the engine bay. The sticker also shows the model, paint and trim codes. Ask the owner for the log book and check the details match the car you're looking at.

So, should you stay or go?
This really is down to the price being asked and whether it corresponds with the condition and mileage of the car. For example, if the car is being sold at market rate for a model in good condition, and you find a dent or scratch on the bodywork, this could be an issue. If things seem okay so far, then it's time for a more in-depth look.

8 Key points
– where to look for problems

Bodywork

Look for signs of accident damage; an orange peel-like finish or poor colour matching are obvious giveaways. The nose and windscreen of the MINI are quite upright by design so check for stonechips. MINIs are well rust-proofed from the factory and even the oldest are just over 10 years old, so there should be no evidence of rust. Expect kerb damage on larger wheels, but this shouldn't be excessive and tyre wear should be even.

These marks in the paint suggest poor preparation for a previous respray.

The MINI's upright nose is prone to damage from stonechips.

Why is this 2002 Cooper fitted with a later front bumper and headlights? Has it been involved in an accident?

Interior

Expect rattles, especially on early cars but the trim and plastics should all be in good condition. Watch for splitting, sagging front seats and scuffing on the side bolsters of the sports versions. Check for excessive wear on the steering wheel, pedals and gearshift – does it correspond with the mileage? Finally make sure all the electrics work – standard or not.

Scuffs are common on the side bolsters of the supportive sports seats.

MINI interiors improved over the course of production, as this 2006 Cooper S shows.

A dirty engine bay like this could be a sign of trouble.

Service history

A full official MINI dealer service history is preferable, but with so many cars out of the TLC servicing scheme, a mixture of dealer and specialist stamps is fine. Basically, the more proof of regular maintenance, such as receipts and stamps in the service book, the better.

Engine

The engine bay should be in good condition, clean and free from corrosion. Check carefully for oil and other fluid leaks.

Underbody

How secure is the front bumper and what is the condition of the lower air dam? Both should be securely attached, as they're quite low and are easily damaged by speed humps and kerbs. Also, check the condition of the exhaust for signs of damage from grounding.

9 Serious evaluation
– 60 minutes for years of enjoyment

Score each section as follows: 4 = excellent; 3 = good; 2 = average; 1 = poor
The totting up procedure is detailed at the end of the chapter. Be realistic in your marking!

Exterior

Most MINI owners tend to look after their cars, and a brief walk around the car should give you a good idea of what to check. Many are owned by enthusiasts, or people who have bought the car and become enthusiasts. This means that there are plenty of top condition, well-equipped cars available. If the car you're looking at has tired bodywork, then you might not want to go any further with the inspection.

Bodywork and panels
Start at the front of the car and look for damage to the leading edge of the bonnet (hood) and front bumper; the number of chips should be consistent with the age and mileage of the MINI but shouldn't be excessive. How deep are they? If they've gone right down to the metal and are not treated, corrosion could develop.

Move on to the side of the car. The MINI has no side protection and is susceptible to car park 'dings.' Look at the panels from different angles to check for these. Check the rear quarter panels especially carefully, as any damage here is particularly difficult to repair.

The front edge of the roof can also suffer from some stonechip damage. If the car you're looking at is an early model with the sunroof, check for small dents around the rear edge of the glass. There were some problems with the mechanism here on 2001/2002 models; these were

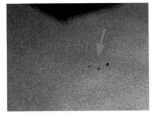

Check for stonechip damage to the bodywork; if left it could go rusty.

Rear quarter damage like this is difficult and costly to repair.

Rear lip spoiler for 2001-06 Chili pack R50 MINI.

the subject of a recall and should have been rectified. If not, ask why not.

Move on to the boot, open it and check the condition of the rubber. Look for corrosion, but also check whether the cabling for the third rear brakelight has rubbed the paint, as this is another potential corrosion risk. If the car has a spoiler, check it's correctly fitted.

Finally, are the bumpers secure? Expect some flexing, but if there's more movement it could signify past crash damage and broken fixings. Is it fitted with the more attractive Chrome Line exterior pack (standard on One and Cooper with Pepper and Chili option packs), what sort of condition are the chrome inserts in? If the MINI you're viewing has a bodykit, check how it's fitted, as any extra drill holes in the bodywork are a potential rust risk.

Chrome bumper inserts were an option, or fitted as standard with the Chili pack.

Paint 4 3 2 1

The paint code is located on the vehicle identification number (VIN) which is stamped on a sticker on the right-hand side front chassis leg. The colour will also be listed on the vehicle registration certificate (V5C). Questions should be asked if the code doesn't match the colour of the car. MINIs are well-painted from the factory, with standards up to those of a BMW. The finish and colour should be the same all over (apart from Cooper and Cooper S models with white and black roofs); any differences in shade or finish maybe due to crash repairs, so ask the owner for more details. Check under the carpets and/or boot floor for evidence of a respray, as these are areas often overlooked.

Cooper and Cooper S models were available with white or black roofs.

Shut lines 4 3 2 1

The curvy styling of the MINI makes it hard to hide poor panel gaps, so any problems should be easy to spot. Start at the front with the bonnet. Are the gaps even, where it meets the bumper and the scuttle? If not, this could suggest that the bonnet has been off the car – ask why. Check the condition of the window seals – even on the oldest MINI they should be free of moss and press firmly against the window. This is particularly important as the

Paint code is part of the Vehicle Identification Number, which is fixed to the right-hand front chassis leg.

MINI has frameless doors, so the seals need to be in good in order to keep the rain out.

The rear bumper should also have an even gap with the body, and flush with the rear arches. If not, check to see if the bumper fixings have been damaged. If there's a bodykit fitted, check for unsightly gaps.

Exterior trim [4] [3] [2] [1]

The plastic wheelarch trims and bumpers are a key part of the MINI's design, so make sure they are secure and free from damage. Pay particular attention to the arch trims as they can work loose and scratch the paintwork.

The shut lines on this bonnet are not uniform and suggest poor repairs.

Wipers [4] [3] [2] [1]

The MINI has two front wipers with three different speeds and a manual spray button that triggers the wipers. There's also a rear windscreen wiper to aid visibility, although this is not fitted to the rare, lightweight GP edition. The wipers should all move across the glass without smearing, otherwise they will probably need replacing.

Spoilers [4] [3] [2] [1]

Only first generation R53 Cooper S versions were fitted with a rear spoiler as standard. However, a simple rear lip or even the Aero kit spoiler were a popular option on the R50 One and Cooper, so don't be surprised to find a spoiler fitted. This was rectified on later R56 Cooper versions, with a deeper rear lip as standard.

Plastic arch trims can work loose and scratch the paint.

The most extreme rear spoiler fitted to a MINI has to be the limited edition GP's unique MINI Challenge-style wing. With the centre piece made from carbon fibre, it's rare but difficult and expensive to replace, so make sure it's not damaged.

There's also the chance that the standard rear spoiler might have been replaced with other more extreme aftermarket versions; just make sure it's securely fitted and that you like the look of it.

Even the most extreme rear spoiler on a MINI will not affect rear visibility, as the spoiler fits around the top part of the rear window.

More distinctive rear lip spoiler for the R56 MINI.

R50 pre-face-lift halogen headlights.

R50 pre-face-lift xenon headlights.

Face-lift R50 halogen headlights should be brighter because of improved reflectors.

Alien-like, projector-style face-lift xenon headlights for R50 MINI models.

The biggest change for second generation R56 MINI headlights was the indictor unit, which was moved from the bumper.

Customising MINI headlights is a popular modification; the internals of this xenon headlight have been painted.

Lights

Two types of front headlights were available on first and second generation MINIs: standard halogen or the optional and more powerful xenon headlights. There were two types of halogens and xenons, one for pre-face-lift and one for post-face-lift cars.

MINI knew that despite looking good, the performance of the original lights was poor. They tried to resolve this problem with revised headlamps for all models from 2004. Face-lifted standard headlights can be identified by the circular reflectors. More obvious are the second generation xenon lights which look alien-like, with the projector-style main bulb and its eyelash-like detail.

Swapping the headlights on a MINI isn't unheard of, but is a less popular modification. Owners have been known to upgrade to the more powerful xenons, so check with the owner and make sure that any upgrade has been done correctly. Changing the headlights for aftermarket versions is possible but not popular; instead many owners are customising the standard headlights. Known as a Joey mod, it basically involves carefully taking the headlight unit apart and colour-coding or painting the internals of the headlight – and can look really good, if it's done well.

The same choices of halogen and xenon lights were also offered for second generation R56 models. The biggest change here was moving the indicators from the bumper into the headlights.

Rear light cluster from a pre-face-lift R50 MINI in good condition.

Aftermarket rear lights are a popular modification; check out these LED versions.

Clear rear light clusters on MINIs improve the rear's appearance.

R56 second generation rear lights might look similar to first generation ones, but are completely different and much brighter.

Face-lifted R50 rear MINI light cluster includes larger reflectors and reversing lights.

Chromed driving lights are a popular accessory, but need looking after, especially through the winter as the finish is prone to pitting from road salt.

Like the headlights, there were two different styles of rear lights for first generation MINIs. The first set on models from 2001 to 2004 are a more simple design, with a round indicator in the centre, foglight above, and the brake/tail light below. There's also a small reversing light at the bottom of the rear bumper.

It was all change for the face-lifted rear lights after 2004, as the indicators became smaller and moved to the top, the brake/tail light grew with a much larger reflector and a reversing light was squeezed into the corner. With reversing lights fitted in the rear light clusters, obviously the bumper-mounted light was redundant, so this was turned red to become the foglight.

Changing the rear lights is a popular modification on first generation cars, with MINI even offering expensive clear or part clear versions as accessories. If the car you're viewing is fitted with clear rear light clusters, make sure there's some sort of red reflector fitted to the rear bumper, as they are illegal without, and won't pass the MoT. MINI actually removed these lights from sale for a while, as dealers weren't fitting the reflectors.

Also popular are non-standard aftermarket rear lights; if these are fitted to a car you're looking at, firstly see if you like them. If not, check if the owner has the originals so that they can be refitted at a later date. Also, ensure they're fitted correctly and that the wiring isn't suspect.

R56 MINIs again have completely different rear lights. There are fewer choices for modification, with just the option of clear indicator versions available. On the plus side, these were the brightest rear lights until the change to LED rear lights at the end of 2010.

Convertible roof

If you're looking at buying a convertible MINI, the first thing to check is the condition of the fabric roof. The roof should be free of tears, but also check for evidence of rubbing around the rear of the hood where it folds. This is a known problem with early cars and should have been rectified by the dealer at the time.

The MINI's roof is operated in two stages; the first is almost like a sunroof, as only part of the roof folds back over the front passenger compartment, the second is where the roof completely folds. Try to raise and lower the roof a couple of times to make sure it works correctly.

The convertible roof should be free of rips and the glass free from damage.

Glass

The MINI's design means the windscreen is quite upright and prone to stonechips. A couple of minor chips are acceptable, but if the car you're looking at has bigger chips or worse, a crack, then factor in the cost of a new screen (approximately ●x300) when negotiating a price. Both first and second generation MINIs were offered with an optional heated front screen; it's a rare but attractive option.

Right: 17in S-spoke alloy wheels were fitted to R50 Cooper S models with the Chili pack.

Above: Standard 16in five-star alloy wheels on the Cooper, with Dunlop tyres.

Above: Factory alloy wheels were also available in white finish. The Cooper S on the left is fitted with standard 16in X-lite wheels. (Courtesy MINI UK)

Finally, the rear window is glass and heated; make sure it's not damaged and that the heating element is working.

Wheels and tyres

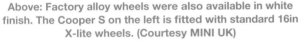

The MINI One or One D weren't fitted with alloys as standard and instead have 15in steel wheels with trims. These are rare, as alloy wheels were a popular option, so don't be surprised if they're upgraded to the 15in alloys of the Pepper Pack.

The Cooper had 15in alloy wheels as standard, with a choice of different styles, both before and after the 2004 facelift. There are more alloy wheel options for the Cooper, with the sportier Chili pack adding the popular 16in five-star style. Also available as an option were 17in S-spoke and latterly Bullet style alloys.

Above: Bullet-style 17in alloy wheels fitted to face-lifted R50 Cooper and Cooper S models. (Courtesy MINI UK)

Move up to the range-topping Cooper S and 16in X-lite alloy wheels were standard, but many buyers were tempted by the high-value Chili pack which included the sought-after 17in alloys. The rare Cooper S GP limited edition is fitted with unique 18in wheels, the biggest alloys yet fitted to a new MINI.

Unique, lightweight Cooper S GP 18in four-spoke alloy wheels.

All factory alloys for Cooper and Cooper S are available in silver or white finishes, the latter only available with a white roof.

The 15in alloys take a 175/65 R15 tyre, usually Pirellis. The 16in alloys are fitted with 195/55 R16 tyres, which came from the factory with Dunlop run-flats. Finally, the 17in alloys are fitted with 205/45 R 17 tyres, which again were Dunlop run-flats. However, don't be surprised if a car you're looking at with the 16in or 17in wheels isn't fitted with run-flats, as their exaggerating effect on the already hard ride has made them unpopular with owners and enthusiasts.

There was also a large choice of alloys in various styles and sizes from the accessories catalogue. Check with the owner to find out if the wheels on the car you're viewing are the same ones it left the factory or dealer with.

R56 MINIs were offered with the same choices of alloy wheel size, but offered in different styles.

On top of this there's a huge choice of non-standard alloys, so you'll probably view cars with all sorts of wheel and tyre combinations – just make sure you're happy with the style and condition.

Wheel condition ⁤ 4️⃣ 3️⃣ 2️⃣ 1️⃣

A quick look over the wheels should give you an idea of their overall condition. Kerbing and scratching can be repaired, but might be a sign of misuse or suspension problems. Look at the spokes to check for chips, and around the studs for lacquer damage that will cause corrosion. If you can't see enough from the outside, don't be afraid to have a look underneath with a torch if necessary.

Tyre condition ⁤ 4️⃣ 3️⃣ 2️⃣ 1️⃣

Look at the tread depth of all four tyres – are they wearing evenly? If not, this could be down to incorrect tyre pressures, but could also be caused by damaged suspension, wheel misalignment or even crash damage. Also, check the sidewalls of the tyres for any splits and cuts caused by hard kerbing.

Suspension bushes, lower control arm bushes, universal joints ⁤ 4️⃣ 3️⃣ 2️⃣ 1️⃣

Dampers on all first generation MINIs seem to be good quality and last well, even with high mileage. However, if you hear a clinking noise from either the front or back suspension, it could mean that the top mounting bushes are worn out. It's less common at the front, but the front anti-roll bar links should also be checked as a precaution. Examine this by taking the wheel(s) off the ground using a jack or ramp. Pull and push the wheel and listen for noises.

Worn lower control arms can affect all models. If on the test drive the car feels like it's wandering and suddenly veers off course, then the lower control arm bushes may be failing. Cheap to replace, but made more involved by the fact that the subframe has to be dropped. This is not a DIY-friendly job.

Noises at the front could mean worn anti-roll bar bushes.

Universal joints are the next area to check. Start the engine and turn the steering wheel to lock while stationary.

If you hear a banging noise from the steering column, this could indicate a problem with the universal joint which is difficult and expensive to fix.

The R56 generation is still too new for any of these faults to have developed.

Interior
The interior of the MINI, like the exterior, is one of the main attractions of this car. It's both unique and stylish, but the interior plastics vary in quality and some scratch and mark very easily, spoiling the effect. However quality improved right through production of the first generation MINI. There was far more choice to customise the interior of the R56 car and quality took a major step forward.

With such a huge variety of seats, trims and dashboard finishes, expect to see a wide range of interiors, differing in look and feel. Just make sure it's in a condition that corresponds with the mileage.

With such a large choice of interior trims and finishes, no two MINI interiors should ever be the same.

Some interior plastics on the first generation R50 MINI mark and scratch easily.

Seats

One and Cooper models were fitted with standard seats, although the Cooper benefits from sportier trim. They are comfortable enough, but more side support would be welcome on the faster, sharper handling Cooper. Moving up to the Chili pack on Cooper and Cooper S models, more supportive sports seats were fitted as standard, trimmed in half-leather. These models also have more choice of interior trim combinations. Full leather trim was a popular option again on Cooper and Cooper S models, the latter looks particularly good with the coloured inserts. Watch

Sparco sports seats complete with JCW badging (Courtesy MINI UK).

out for (unpopular) textured leather on Cooper models. Favoured front seats are the Recaros, which were fitted as standard on the Cooper S GP, and available as an option on Cooper and Cooper S models from 2005. Sparco JCW rally-style front seats were an expensive but popular accessory. They certainly make the interior feel more special and exclusive.

The second generation MINI's interior is all about personalisation; there are two types of front seats: standard and sports. Go for the sports seats and there's the choice of fabric, standard leather, a mix of both or leather lounge trim. The standard seats fitted to Salt and Pepper pack Coopers are a big improvement over the first generation cars as they offer better side support. Of the sports seats on the Cooper and Cooper S models, the classiest has to be the lounge leather seats; their design looks more classic with the contrasting piping.

Carpets ⓸ ⓷ ⓶ ⓵

Black, blue or grey and great quality, but they shouldn't be worn, as the majority of cars should still have the carpet mats that were part of the pack options. The carpet can be lifted, although with difficulty, and the wiring for the rear speakers and CD auto changer can be found between the floorpan and the carpet. Does it look like it's been removed before? If so, ask why. R56 MINIs were available with black carpets only.

Headlining/sunroof ⓸ ⓷ ⓶ ⓵

There are two sun visors at the front, with flip-up illuminated vanity mirrors. These can be moved to shield the door windows but face-lift models were fitted with an extra visor near the driver's side grab handle. Above every seat except the driver's there's a coat grip/handle. Mostly grey, an anthracite headlining was offered as an option on Cooper and Cooper S versions, but is standard on the GP. The headlining should be in excellent condition, but check for water staining on models fitted with the grey headlining and sunroof.

The only change for the second generation MINI is that the central courtesy light moves to the front of the car in a bank of retro-styled switches, mimicking those at the bottom of the dashboard.

Chromed door handles are a standard feature on all MINIs. (Courtesy MINI UK)

Door cards/keys/handles ⓸ ⓷ ⓶ ⓵

All MINIs have chunky, chrome, retro-styled door handles with a push-button mechanism. Key-operated remote central locking is standard on all models, and will operate the alarm, where fitted. The central locking can also be operated by the key on both doors. As a security measure, the key will also close the electric front windows if they're left open. The two front doors hold the front speakers and tweeters. If the car you're looking at has distinctive turbine-like grilles clearly branded Harmon Kardon, then it has the expensive and powerful speaker upgrade. The door cards will be either grey, black or blue, depending on the interior trim.

Apart from slight changes to the design, the door cards and handles are the same for the second generation MINI.

Electric windows

The electric front windows are operated by rocker switches in the centre console. If you're looking at a convertible, the controls for the rear windows are in the roof at the front. The windows are frameless and should drop slightly when the door is open. Look at the condition of the window rubbers, as this could result in more wind noise around the front windows.

Steering wheel

MINI One models were fitted with an unpopular plastic version of the standard-fit single spoke air-bagged steering wheel, and many were specified with optional leather finish. Move up to a Cooper and the same steering wheel was fitted, but this time it was leather-trimmed. A thicker sports steering wheel with thumb grips was fitted as standard to the Cooper S and was included as standard for Pepper and Chili pack versions of the Cooper. A multi-function version of the same steering wheel with buttons for the stereo and cruise control was also available. In 2003, a three-spoke steering wheel was added, with a similar multi-function version fitted to face-lifted Chili Cooper S versions. A suede-trimmed JCW version was an expensive, but attractive accessory.

Later, three-spoke multi-function steering wheel for R50, R52 and R53 MINIs has circular buttons for the stereo and cruise control.

Base R56 Cooper and Cooper S models were fitted with a re-designed version of the single spoke steering wheel that's mostly black, with silver detailing for the spokes. It's too thin and doesn't look particularly sporty, so no wonder most cars are fitted with the optional three-spoke sports or multi-function steering wheels.

The steering column on both MINI generations is adjustable for rake and reach, with the release lever under the column.

2005 R50 Cooper speedo with the warning lights on. This car has the optional chrome pack.

Rev counter, where fitted, is mounted on the steering column and houses the trip computer.

My, how you've grown! The speedo on the second generation MINI is dinner plate-sized and is where the stereo lives. (Courtesy MINI UK)

Instrument panel ④ ③ ② ①

The main instruments are in the centre of the dash, finished in silver (grey on the GP); consisting of a circular speedo with petrol and temperature gauges on either side. A steering column mounted rev counter is standard on the Cooper and Cooper S, and optional on the One, although it's rare to find a car where it's not fitted. The rev counter is also home to the trip computer, where fitted. If you're looking at a car with the optional sat nav, the screen is where the instruments usually are, and the speedo moves alongside the rev counter on the steering column. A chrono pack, with larger temperature and petrol gauges was available from the 2004 facelift and like the sat nav, the speedo and rev counter were moved to the steering column.

It was all change for the R56 MINI, as the speedo is the central point of a bolder dashboard and has grown to dinner plate size. There's no longer a temperature gauge, the petrol gauge is now a circular band of lights and the bottom displays radio or CD information. The rev counter is still mounted on the steering column, but now houses the mileage, trip and warning lights. A more advanced DVD-based sat nav was an expensive option and like before, the screen sits where the speedo is usually found. However, there's now a slim speedo around the edge. The controls for the sat nav on both generations are between the gearlever and handbrake.

Centre console ④ ③ ② ①

The BMW MINI's centre console design might differ by generation, but the basic format remains the same. On first generation cars, underneath the speedo, there's the Boost or Wave stereos (depending on model and option pack). Below that, there are circular controls for the ventilation (air-conditioning or climate control options). At the bottom of the centre console, there's a row of rocker switches to operate amongst other things the electric windows. These switches like the central

MINI centre console with CVT gearshift. Note the rocker switches below the climate controls, which mimic those fitted to the Classic Mini. (Courtesy MINI UK)

speedo are designed to echo the design of the Issigonis original.

The centre console on R56 MINIs is a radical departure from the first generation. It's much slimmer, giving more knee room. Move on to the stereo and it's a fully-integrated radio/CD unit, with the CD slot and volume control mounted below the massive speedo. Then there are the controls for the air-conditioning or climate control (again dependent on model and options), which are now designed to resemble the MINI's winged badge. The console is completed by a similar bank of rocker switches. iPod and MP3 fans are better catered for in the second generation cars, as there's a jack point hidden in the centre console.

Gauges

Apart from those already listed, any other gauges fitted to a MINI will be of the non-standard variety. The MINI accessories catalogue offered an extra set of gauges, which fitted under the rocker switches, in the space between the centre console and the transmission tunnel. Later, a JCW LED rev limiter and shift light was offered as an accessory. It fits to the top of the dashboard above the speedo. Aftermarket gauges will probably be fitted in a pod on the A-pillar; whether they are of any use really depends on how modified the engine of the car you're looking at is – they are usually fitted for a reason. Look closely at how they've been installed, and check any wiring very carefully.

Pedals

Both generations of One and Cooper pedals are covered by rubber grips that don't look particularly racy. Sportier aluminium pedals with rubber grips are standard on all Cooper S models. Owners of early Ones and Coopers may have fitted aftermarket pedals, so make sure that they've been correctly secured and check for wear and tear. There is a footrest to the left of the pedals.

Airbags

Driver, passenger and front seat airbags were fitted as standard on all MINI models, with side curtain airbags available as an option.

Boot (trunk) 4 3 2 1
The MINI's boot catch is via a solenoid underneath the boot handle. There is an internal light on the right-hand side that turns on when the boot is opened. If a CD auto changer is fitted on first generation models, it's usually on the left-hand side.

Spare wheel 4 3 2 1
Due to a lack of boot space, there's no standard spare wheel on MINI models. Instead, all cars except those fitted with runflat tyres, had what was called a MINI Motability System. This

Chromed boot catch and optional parking distance sensors on this 2005 Cooper.

consisted of a tub of sealant, which should be pumped into the tyre, together with a compressor to inflate it. A space saver wheel was offered as an option on both MINI generations – this is fitted under the boot (trunk) floor.

Fuel filler 4 3 2 1
The earliest recall was for a static discharge risk whilst refuelling; this caused quite a few MINIs to go up in smoke and meant that many of the first customers had to wait for their cars, due for delivery on September 1 2001. All early cars should be repaired and fitted with an earthing strip, so check with the seller and service history to make sure this has been done.

All MINI One and Cooper models have a body-coloured fuel flap on the left-hand side of the car. Cooper S models differ by having a chrome-look flap, but these are an easy modification, so One and Cooper S versions could have a chromed fuel cap too.

Chrome-look fuel cap is standard on the Cooper S, but can be easily retro-fitted to a One or Cooper.

Mechanicals
Under the bonnet 4 3 2 1
There's a lot going on in a relatively small space; first generation R50 One and Cooper models are dominated by the top of the Tritec engine, with the yellow highlighted dipstick and radiator at the front and the sparkplug pack, coolant bottle and battery at the back. Move up to a R53 Cooper S and it's all change again, as the top of the engine is dominated by the intercooler for the supercharger and all the tubing for the induction system. The battery moves to the boot and the dipstick to the right-hand side of the engine.

The standard 1.6-litre and 1.6-litre turbo engines in second generation cars are basically in the same place, but the front end is completely re-designed and the bonnet is no longer of the clamshell variety. The headlights are fixed at the front, and the coolant and windscreen washer bottles have moved to the front of the engine

Clean underside of a 2006 R56 Cooper bonnet.

R56 Cooper S engine with the turbo at the front and the induction system at the back. (Courtesy MINI UK)

bay. The yellow dipstick on both engines has now moved to the right-hand side. The Cooper S is identified by the front-mounted turbocharger.

Check on early models that the bonnet padding hasn't rubbed the paint away, causing a potential rust risk.

④ ③ ② ①
Engine mounts

Check closely, as they will wear out over time. A common failure on first generation MINIs is the right-hand side circular oil-filled engine mount. It's easy to spot problems, as it will leak oil all over the front chassis leg. A replacement can cost ●x65.

④ ③ ② ①
Chassis number

The 17 digit vehicle identification number (VIN) can be found on the right-hand side front chassis leg in the engine bay. The VIN is also marked in the right-hand corner of the front windscreen.

R56 models also have their VIN stamped in the top of the right-hand suspension strut.

Right-hand engine mount is a known failure on first generation cars; check for oil leaks like this.

The MINI's VIN is visible through the front windscreen.

Standard R50 Cooper exhaust with its 'Coke can' style exhaust finisher.

Twin centre exhausts are fitted to all Cooper S models; this is a less restrictive JCW one.

Supercharger 4 3 2 1

Generally, the Eaton M45 blower fitted to the first generation R53 Cooper S doesn't give problems, but watch for slipping supercharger belts caused by failing tensioners. If the engine is cold, you should hear squeaking from the belt. If there are problems, the supercharger will sound generally rough. A tensioner kit from BMW costs ●x120.

Exhaust system 4 3 2 1

R50 One and Cooper and second generation R56 Cooper models are fitted with a side exit exhaust and a coke can-style exhaust finisher. All Cooper S models on the other hand, have a twin centre exit exhaust. All the standard exhausts are supposedly made from stainless steel, but they do rot, peeling back in layers like an onion. So, if the car you're looking at is over seven years old, check the condition of the back box carefully. Also, first generation manifolds can split, but this will be obvious on start-up as it would sound like a tractor.

JCW and non-standard sports exhaust upgrades are louder, so make sure you can live with the extra noise.

4 3 2 1
Electronic Control Unit (ECU)

Remaps are a popular way to liberate more performance from the BMW MINI. Particularly on the 90bhp One, which when mapped can give Cooper-rivalling performance. Expert advice is recommended for remapping and it will affect the insurance, so look for supporting documents for any work done.

Spark plugs 4 3 2 1

Difficult to change; thankfully the spark plugs last up to 50,000 miles.

Gaskets   4   3   2   1

There are two gaskets to watch out for with the MINI; the first that affects both generations is the rocker cover gasket. It's a known failure because of the way the engine leans back and puts pressure on the back of this gasket; it then degrades and results in oil leaks down the back and sides of the engine. These are not easy to spot, so get your head under the bonnet and look down the back of the engine. If you can't do this, use your hands but only when the engine is cold. Not a difficult job, the part costs approximately ●x19 and should just take an hour's labour.

The second is the sump gasket on first generation cars; get underneath and look for general leaks and moisture from the bottom of the engine. Again, the gasket itself isn't expensive at approximately ●x20, but the air-conditioning pump has to be moved, resulting in three to four hours labour at a specialist. It will be a lot more at dealers.

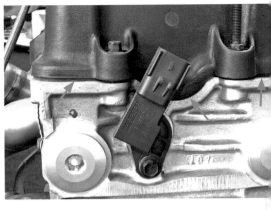

Rocker cover gasket is a known failure point due to the engine's angle. (Courtesy Lohen)

Suspension   4   3   2   1

The MINI's front suspension consists of MacPherson struts with a lower lateral arm. The rear suspension is more sophisticated, with a version of the multi-link Z-axle. This helps to give the MINI its keen handling.

The MINI's suspension is strong, reliable and generally gives few problems. However, parts do wear out so it's worth checking the following items. Firstly, check the condition of the dampers. They last well, but if you're looking at a car that's over seven years old they will be past their best.

Suspension top mounts were the cause of early cars' wayward steering; a front strut brace has been added here.

Modified cars should have supporting paperwork detailing what's been done and by whom.

About 35mm is the norm, any more than that, up to 50mm, and you need to find out who did the work, and with what parts. If it's on standard suspension, it's likely to be tired.

Strut braces ④ ③ ② ①
Not standard, but a popular modification, especially on Cooper S models. Front braces are often fitted by owners aiming to improve the handling. Fitting a brace under the bonnet of a MINI is tight work, so make sure it's fitted correctly and hasn't damaged items such as the bonnet.

This car is fitted with a JCW strut brace that further stiffens the suspension and sharpens handling.

Security systems ④ ③ ② ①
All first generation MINIs were fitted with a category 1 immobiliser, with an alarm, standard on models fitted with the Chili pack. Some cars will have been fitted with upgraded aftermarket systems; check they work correctly and there are receipts for the work done. All R56 models have an immobiliser and alarm as standard.

Heat shields ④ ③ ② ①
Made from aluminum, they stand the heat very well and won't rust. They can work loose though, so listen for squeaks underneath.

Steering rack ④ ③ ② ①
Steering is via a rack and pinion system. Most models having 2.5 turns lock to lock. There are no problems reported with the steering racks of both first and second generation MINIs, but expect general wear and tear.

Exhaust heat shields can work loose and rattle.

Clutch ④ ③ ② ①
There are generally no issues with the MINI clutch, apart from wear and tear.

Gearbox ④ ③ ② ①
The R50 MINI One and Cooper's 5-speed gearbox is called the Midland unit and started life in Peugeots and Citroëns, before being fitted in the Rover version of the Metro. It has a slick, short throw, but gave reliability problems from the start of production. BMW replaced the Midland unit with one from German gearbox supplier

R53 Cooper S fuse box under the bonnet, next to the induction system.

Gertrag after the 2004 face-lift. More mechanical in feel than the original, but reliability is much improved.

MINI also offered two types of automatic transmission for R50 Cooper and R53 Cooper S models. Firstly there's a conventional CVT transmission for the One and Cooper; this isn't recommended as there have been reports of total failure even at low mileage and high mileage models will be the worst affected. The second option introduced for the 2005 model year Cooper S, was the Aisin 6-speed automatic transmission, to appeal to the American market. Auto versions of the Cooper S are slower, and despite the steering wheel-mounted paddles, the car can sometimes override the manual control from time to time.

The second generation car differs from the first in that the Cooper, like the Cooper S, is fitted with a Gertrag 6-speed manual gearbox. Cooper and Cooper S models were still offered with the optional Aisin 6-speed automatic.

Close-up of the Cooper S 6-speed gearbox lever.

Cooling   4   3   2   1

Check the thermostat housing on early One and Cooper models, as these can fail causing coolant leaks. There should be coolant in the expansion tank and it should be blue in colour. If not, it could be a matter of just topping it up, but it could also indicate a leak or in worst cases an indicator of head gasket trouble.

The coolant tank can leak; look for staining around the side.

Battery   4   3   2   1

MINIs don't like short journeys, as the battery doesn't get a proper charge. If you're looking at a car that's between four to five years old, and it's really lazy to start-up, budget for a new battery.

R53 Cooper S battery, located in the boot.

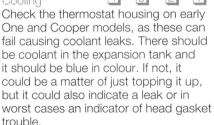

The second MINI fuse box can be found in the front footwell.

The oil breather pipe on top of the engine can go soft and leak. (Courtesy Lohen)

JCW brake upgrade includes bigger front discs and red calipers.

Electrics ④ ③ ② ①

The BMW MINI has two fuse boxes; one under the bonnet and the other under the dashboard. There are no known problems with first or second generation cars.

Hoses ④ ③ ② ①

Not really a problem. However, check the oil breather pipe at the top of the engine on first generation cars, as over time the rubber absorbs oil, goes soft and leaks. There are plenty of other hoses in the engine bay linked up to the requisite components with metal clips. Check these for cracks, softness and leaks.

Brakes ④ ③ ② ①

Generally fine, apart from wear and tear. Check the condition of the brake discs first, they should be shiny and smooth, but may have rust if parked for a while – this should come off with use. Expect some corrosion around the disc, especially if the car has lived outside. If the discs are scored or rusty they will need replacement – performance will be compromised, because there's less surface for the brake pad to grip. If the brake discs have a blue tinge to them, they might be distorted due to overheating.

Uprated brakes are a common feature of modified first generation Cooper S', as they lack stopping power and are prone to fading. BMW offered an upgrade in the form of a JCW kit, which is fitted as standard to

the GP. It's identified by the red
front calipers and larger 294mm
front discs. Other non-standard
brake options can be fitted,
including the R56 Brembo kit
which is now standard on the
current performance range-
topper, the JCW.

Test drive
Cold start ⁤⁤⁤⁤ 4 3 2 1
Turn the key (or press the start button on second generation R56 models); don't
use high revs (above 3000rpm) until the engine is fully warmed through. Any blue or
white smoke on start-up could indicate engine or turbo problems.

Warning lights ⁤⁤⁤⁤ 4 3 2 1
The warning lights should come
on when the key is inserted
and half-turned, and then go
off when the engine is started.
However, on first generation
cars, look at the speedo: is
the airbag light still on? This is
a common fault, caused by a
wiring loom that runs under the
front seats. It can be due to
something as simple as the front
seat mechanism being pulled too
hard when getting in the back of
the car.

**Warning lights should go off when the
engine is started.**

Clutch operation ⁤⁤⁤⁤ 4 3 2 1
Is there a grinding noise that goes away when the clutch is engaged? If so, it
could be that the clutch release bearing is noisy. If you're in a R53 Cooper S and
there are similar grinding noises when you select gears, this could indicate a failing
dual-mass flywheel. Tread carefully, as this is an expensive repair – budget around
●x400 at a specialist.

Gearbox operation ⁤⁤⁤⁤ 4 3 2 1
Make sure in any early Midland gearbox-equipped R50 One and Cooper models
that all the gears are easily selected, and listen for odd whining noises, or a
crunchy gear change. A re-conditioned gearbox is probably the most cost-effective
solution, and is probably the cheapest route compared to going to a dealer. With
the gearbox out it would be foolish not to replace the clutch; expect to pay around
●x700 for both.

6-speed R56 gearbox in excellent condition, shown alongside the exhaust downpipe.

Steering feel ☑ 4 ☑ 3 ☑ 2 ☑ 1

Problems with the power steering are as common as gearbox problems on early MINIs. If the steering feels rough, weights up oddly, or is imprecise when making turns, it's probably the power steering pump at fault. Budget approximately ●x350 to fix the pump at a specialist.

If you also hear a knocking noise when making left or right turns on the test drive, this could indicate worn lower ball joints, trackrod ends or driveshafts.

Brakes operation ☑ 4 ☑ 3 ☑ 2 ☑ 1

The rear calipers can seize together on the rear discs. You can usually identify this on the test drive by judders or general vibrations from the brakes.

Noises ☑ 4 ☑ 3 ☑ 2 ☑ 1

Start the engine and listen: are there any unusual noises? Can you hear a rattling noise from the top or bottom end? If the rattle is coming from the top end it could be that the hydraulic tappets are on their way out, or that the timing chain needs tensioning. Rattles from the bottom end are more serious, and could indicate that the engine has run out of oil at some point. Walk away if there are any apparent engine problems, as there's such a wide choice of MINIs around.

Performance ☑ 4 ☑ 3 ☑ 2 ☑ 1

Resist the urge to enjoy the engine's performance until it's fully warmed up; on first generation cars this is when the gauge is halfway between hot and cold. All engines should be responsive through the gears. If you're looking at either a first or second generation Cooper S, there should be some supercharger whine or turbo hiss when accelerating. All MINIs' engine performance should impress in the mid-range, yet the car should still be capable in urban environments.

Controls and switches ☑ 4 ☑ 3 ☑ 2 ☑ 1

The controls and switches over both generations of MINI are basically the same and logical. Just make sure they all work, especially the windows, headlights and central locking.

Ramp check ☑ 4 ☑ 3 ☑ 2 ☑ 1

Start at the front, checking the condition of the front subframe and sump. What do the wheels look like from underneath? Are they buckled, chipped or scratched? Could this have been caused by careless driving? What sort of condition are the tyres in; are they wearing evenly? Look at the condition of the arches; is there any damage to support the condition of the wheels? Push and pull the wheels to see whether there's any bearing wear. A whirring, grinding noise could mean they will soon need to be replaced. Look at the condition of the CV boots on the driveshafts, splits or holes in the rubber are a bad sign. Grime and grit will have contaminated the CV joint and a replacement is the only way to fix this.

Then follow the length of the exhaust, checking for rot, leaks and damage caused by careless driving. Also, look for signs of corrosion in the rear subframe and take a look at the condition of the brake lines, as they are made from mild steel and will rust.

R56 Cooper exhaust system shown from back to front.

Evaluation procedure
Add up the total points.
Score: 228 = excellent; 171 = good; 114 = average; 57 = poor.

Cars scoring over 160 will be completely usable and will require only maintenance and care to preserve condition. Cars scoring between 67 and 116 will require some serious work (at much the same cost regardless of score). Cars scoring between 117 and 159 will require very careful assessment of the necessary repair/restoration costs in order to arrive at a realistic value.

10 Auctions
– Sold! Another way to buy your dream

Auction pros & cons
Pros: Prices are generally lower than those of dealers or private sellers, and you might grab a real bargain. Auctioneers have usually established clear title with the seller. At the venue you should be able to see documentation relating to the vehicle.
Cons: You have to rely on a sketchy catalogue description of condition and history. The opportunity to inspect is limited, and you cannot drive the car. Auction cars are often a little below par and may require some work. It's easy to overbid. There is usually a buyer's premium to pay in addition to the auction hammer price.

Which auction?
Auctions by established auctioneers are advertised in car magazines and on the auction houses' websites. A catalogue, or a simple printed list of the lots for auctions might only be available a day or two ahead, though often lots are listed and pictured on auctioneers' websites much earlier. Contact the auction company to ask if previous auction selling prices are available as this is useful information (details of past sales are often available on websites).

Catalogue, entry fee and payment details
When you purchase the catalogue of the vehicles in the auction, it often acts as a ticket allowing two people to attend the viewing days and the auction. Catalogue details tend to be comparatively brief, but will include information such as 'one owner from new, low mileage, full service history', etc. It will also usually show a guide price, giving you some idea of what to expect to pay, and tell you what is charged as a 'Buyer's premium.' The catalogue will also contain details of acceptable forms of payment. At the fall of the hammer an immediate deposit is usually required, the balance payable within 24 hours. If the plan is to pay by cash, there may be a cash limit. Some auctions accept payment by debit card. Sometimes credit or charge cards are acceptable, but often incur an extra charge. A bank draft or bank transfer needs to be arranged in advance with your own bank, as well as with the auction house. No car will be released before all payments are cleared. If delays occur in payment transfers, then storage costs can accrue.

Buyer's premium
A buyer's premium will be added to the hammer price: don't forget this in your calculations. It is not usual for there to be a further state tax, or local tax on the purchase price, and/or on the buyer's premium.

Viewing
In some instances it's possible to view on the day, or days before, as well as in the hours prior to, the auction. Auction officials are available, willing to help out by opening engine and luggage compartments and allowing you to inspect the interior. While the officials may start the engine for you, a test drive is out of the question. Crawling under and around the car as much as you want is permitted, but you can't suggest that the car you are interested in be jacked up, or attempt to do the job yourself. You can also ask to see any documentation available.

Bidding

Before you take part in the auction, decide your maximum bid – and stick to it!

It may take a while for the auctioneer to reach the lot you are interested in, so use that time to observe how other bidders behave. When it's the turn of your car, attract the auctioneer's attention and make an early bid. The auctioneer will then look to you for a reaction every time another bid is made, usually the bids will be in fixed increments until the bidding slows, when smaller increments will often be accepted before the hammer falls. If you want to withdraw from the bidding, make sure the auctioneer understands your intentions – a vigorous shake of the head when he or she looks to you for the next bid should do the trick!

Assuming that you are the successful bidder, the auctioneer will note your card or paddle number, and from that moment on you will be responsible for the vehicle.

If the car is unsold, either because it failed to reach the reserve or because there was little interest, it may be possible to negotiate with the owner, via the auctioneers, after the sale is over.

Successful bid

There are two more points to consider: how to get the car home, and insurance. If you can't drive the car, your own or a hired trailer is one way, another is to have the vehicle shipped using the facilities of a local company. The auction house will also have details of companies specialising in the transfer of cars.

Insurance for immediate cover can usually be purchased on site, but it may be more cost-effective to make arrangements with your own insurance company in advance, and then call to confirm the full details.

eBay & other online auctions

eBay & other online auctions could land you a car at a bargain price, though you'd be foolhardy to bid without examining the car first, something most vendors encourage. A useful feature of eBay is that the geographical location of the car is shown, so you can narrow your choices to those within a realistic radius of home. Be prepared to be outbid in the last few moments of the auction. Remember, your bid is binding and that it will be very, very difficult to get restitution in the case of a crooked vendor fleecing you – caveat emptor!

Be aware that some cars offered for sale in online auctions are 'ghost' cars. Don't part with any cash without being sure that the vehicle does actually exist and is as described (usually pre-bidding inspection is possible).

Auctioneers

Barrett-Jackson www.barrett-jackson.com
Bonhams www.bonhams.com
British Car Auctions (BCA) www.bca-europe.com or www.british-car-auctions.co.uk
Cheffins www.cheffins.co.uk
Christies www.christies.com
Coys www.coys.co.uk
eBay www.ebay.com
H&H www.classic-auctions.co.uk
RM www.rmauctions.com
Shannons www.shannons.com.au
Silver www.silverauctions.com

11 Paperwork
– correct documentation is essential!

The paper trail

Ideally, particularly for older models, cars will come with a portfolio of paperwork, accumulated and passed on by a succession of proud owners. This documentation represents the car's real history, revealing the level of care the MINI has received, how much it's been used, which specialists have worked on it, and dates of major repairs and restorations. All of this information will be priceless to you as the new owner, so be very wary of cars with little paperwork to support their claimed history.

Registration documents

All countries/states have some form of registration for private vehicles, whether it's like the American 'pink slip' system or the British 'log book' system.

It is essential to check that the registration document is genuine, that it relates to the car in question, and that all the vehicle's details are correctly recorded, including chassis/VIN and engine numbers (if these are shown). If you are buying from the previous owner, his or her name and address will be recorded in the document. This will not be the case, however, if you are buying from a dealer.

In the UK the current (Euro-aligned) registration document is named 'V5C', and is printed in coloured sections of blue, green and pink. The blue section relates to the car specification, the green section has details of the new owner, and the pink section is sent to the DVLA in the UK when the car is sold. A small section in yellow deals with selling the car within the motor trade.

In the UK the DVLA will provide details of earlier keepers of the vehicle upon payment of a small fee, and much can be learned in this way.

If the car has a foreign registration there may be expensive and time-consuming formalities to complete. Do you really want the hassle?

Roadworthiness certificate

Most country/state administrations require that vehicles are regularly tested to prove they are safe to use on the public highway, and do not produce excessive emissions. In the UK that test (the 'MoT') is carried out at approved testing stations, for a fee. In the USA the requirement varies, but most states insist on emissions tests every two years as a minimum, and the police are charged with pulling over unsafe-looking vehicles.

In the UK the test is required on an annual basis once a vehicle becomes three years old. Of particular relevance for older cars is that the certificate issued includes the mileage reading recorded at the test date, becoming an independent record of that car's history. Ask the seller if previous certificates are available. Without an MoT, the vehicle should be trailered to its new home, unless you insist that a valid MoT is part of the deal. (Not such a bad idea this, as at least you will know the car was roadworthy on the day it was tested and you don't need to wait for the old certificate to expire before having the test done).

Road licence

The administration of every country/state charges some kind of tax for the use of its road system. The actual form of the 'road licence' and, how it is displayed, varying enormously country to country and state to state.

Whatever the form of the 'road licence', it must relate to the vehicle carrying it and must be present and valid if the car is to be driven on the public highway legally. The value of the licence depends on the length of time it will continue to be valid.

In the UK if a car is untaxed because it has not been used for a period of time, the owner must inform the licensing authorities, otherwise the vehicle's date-related registration number will be lost and there will be a painful amount of paperwork to get it re-registered. Also in the UK, vehicles built before the end of 1972 are provided with 'tax discs' free of charge, but they must still display a valid disc. Car clubs can often provide formal proof that a particular car qualifies for this valuable concession.

Certificates of authenticity

For many makes of collectible car it is possible to get a certificate proving the age and authenticity (eg. engine and chassis numbers, paint colour and trim) of a particular vehicle, these are sometimes called 'Heritage Certificates' and if the car comes with one of these it is a definite bonus. If you want to obtain one, the relevant owners' club is the best starting point.

If the car has been used in European classic car rallies it may have a FIVA (Fédération Internationale des Véhicules Anciens) certificate. The so-called 'FIVA Passport', or 'FIVA Vehicle Identity Card,' enables organisers and participants to recognise whether or not a particular vehicle is suitable for individual events. If you want to obtain such a certificate go to www.fbhvc.co.uk or www.fiva.org. There will be similar organisations in other countries too.

Valuation certificate

Hopefully, the vendor will have a recent valuation certificate, or letter signed by a recognised expert stating how much he, or she, believes the particular car to be worth (such documents, together with photos, are usually needed to get 'agreed value' insurance). Generally these documents should act only as confirmation of your own assessment of the car rather than a guarantee of value, as the expert has probably not seen the car in the flesh. The easiest way to find out how to obtain a formal valuation is to contact the owners' club.

Service history

Often these cars will have been serviced at home by enthusiastic (and hopefully capable) owners for a good number of years. Nevertheless, try to obtain as much service history and other paperwork pertaining to the car as you can. Naturally, dealer stamps, or specialist garage receipts score most points in the value stakes. However, anything helps in the great authenticity game, items like the original bill of sale, handbook, parts invoices and repair bills, adding to the story and the character of the car. Even a brochure correct to the year of the car's manufacture is a useful document and something that could well be hard to locate in future years. If the seller claims that the car has been restored, then expect receipts and other evidence from a specialist restorer.

If the seller claims to have carried out regular servicing, ask what work was completed, when, and seek some evidence of it being carried out. Your assessment of the MINI's overall condition should tell you whether their claims are genuine.

Restoration photographs

If the seller tells you that the car has been restored, then expect to be shown a series of photographs taken while the restoration was under way. Pictures taken at various stages, and from various angles, should help you gauge the thoroughness of the work. If you buy the car, ask if you can have all the photographs, as they form an important part of the vehicle's history. It's surprising how many sellers are happy to part with their car and accept your cash, but want to hang on to their photographs! In the latter event, you may be able to persuade the vendor to get a set of copies made.

12 What's it worth?
– let your head rule your heart

If you have used the marking system in chapter 9 you'll know what the car's condition is, even if you're not sure of its value.

Check out magazines and websites with regularly updated price guides, these are a valuable tool for buyers and sellers. There are also price guides which cover more recent models. What you must remember though, is that the majority of MINI models were fitted with Salt, Pepper and Chili packs that can be difficult to list. Also, watch for cars with modifications that are not mentioned in valuations.

Try to buy the car with the best equipment pack that you can afford. For example, models with packs have desirable extras such as 17in alloy wheels, air-conditioning and half leather trim. JCW modifications on Cooper and Cooper S are desirable and will increase a car's value slightly. However, modifying in MINI circles can get addictive, with owners spending thousands on parts. Unfortunately, these sellers will never get all the money back that they've spent but, if you're buying a MINI to modify, it might make more financial sense to buy a car that has your desired upgrades already.

Some modifications won't appeal to all. If you're unsure, will the seller return the car to standard or supply the standard parts that they removed?

Residual values for all the models featured in this book are falling, with only late limited edition models holding up better.

The first of the second generation R56 MINIs are a better buy if you want more refinement and better build quality, even if they're not as sharp to drive.

Looking for a MINI minter? My best advice is to search out show car sales. Show and Shine is still an important part of the show scene, and you might get a car that looks like it has barely turned a wheel.

Desirable extras
Air-conditioning or a sunroof: cars with either will always be more desirable because there's more chance of selling to a wider market.

Alloy wheels: upgrades are popular, but find out what wheels the car originally came with.

Salt, Pepper and Chili pack options: Chili has much more standard kit than the Salt and Pepper packs

Colour: White, red and black are sought after with white or black roofs.

TLC Pack: any MINI with remaining services as part of the TLC maintenance pack will be worth more.

Undesirable features
Cars with engine modifications and no paperwork to support what's been done; cheap or poorly-fitting body kits; cars with body damage.

Doing the deal
By now, you should have a good idea of the car's overall condition – but is it worth what the seller is asking? Is it worth haggling? Private sellers almost expect this and should respond positively. If you're still unsure, but are still interested in the car, why not arrange an independent mechanical inspection? If the seller has nothing to hide, they shouldn't say no.

13 Do you really want to restore?

– it'll take longer and cost more than you think

With the oldest MINIs just over ten years old, and a plentiful supply of used cars, the question has to be asked – why bother? That's not to say restoration isn't possible, but apart from sought after special edition models, the value of all MINIs is on a downward curve and restoration wouldn't be financially viable.

Either way, you'd have to be a qualified mechanic/technician, as well as having a decent budget, because even secondhand, parts are not cheap.

There might be the odd stored away example that's been locked in a heated garage, but most will be pounding the streets and motorways, or being broken for parts in a breakers yard.

You could return a modified car to standard, original condition, but this could be a lengthy, involved project that, again, may cost more than the car's worth. If you must undertake a project like this, special edition models make more sense. But make sure you have all the original parts, as sourcing parts can be a costly and time-consuming exercise.

Special editions are sought after, but finding some parts is becoming more difficult.

If you must restore, then on top of the mechanical knowledge, you're probably going to need some bodywork skills too.

Have you got the time, space and knowledge to complete such a project? If not, why not save yourself time and trouble and buy a cheap early car in good condition to work on and enjoy?

Complicated electrics left exposed to the elements could cause problems that are expensive to fix.

Returning a modified car to standard condition could cost you more than it's worth.

14 Paint problems
– bad complexion, including dimples, pimples and bubbles

Paint faults generally occur due lack of protection/maintenance, or poor preparation prior to a respray or touch-up. Some of the following conditions may be present in the car you're looking at:

Orange peel

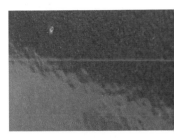

This appears as an uneven paint surface, similar to the skin of an orange. The fault is caused by the failure of atomized paint droplets to flow into each other when they hit the surface. It's sometimes possible to rub out the effect with proprietory paint cutting/rubbing compound, or very fine grades of abrasive paper. A respray may be necessary in severe cases. Consult a bodywork repairer/paint shop for advice on the particular car.

Cracking

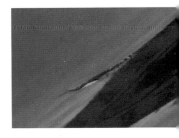

Severe cases are likely to have been caused by too heavy an application of paint (or filler beneath the paint). Also, insufficient stirring of the paint before application can lead to the components being improperly mixed, and cracking can result. Incompatibility with the paint already on the panel can have a similar effect. To rectify the problem it is necessary to rub down the surface to a smooth, sound finish, before respraying the problem area.

Crazing

Sometimes the paint takes on a crazed, rather than a cracked, appearance when the problems mentioned under 'Cracking' are present. This problem can also be caused by a reaction between the underlying surface and the paint. Paint removal and respraying the problem area is usually the only solution.

Blistering

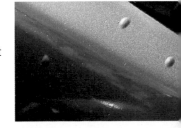

Almost always caused by corrosion of the metal beneath the paint. Usually perforation will be found in the metal, and the damage will often be worse than that suggested by the area of blistering. The metal needs to be repaired before repainting.

Micro blistering

Usually the result of an economy respray, where inadequate heating has allowed moisture to settle on the car before spraying. Consult a paint specialist, but usually damaged paint will have to be removed before partial or full respraying. Can also be caused by car covers that don't 'breathe.'

Peeling

Often a problem with metallic paintwork, when the sealing lacquer becomes damaged, and begins to peel off. Poorly applied paint may also peel. The remedy is to strip and start again!

Fading

Some colours, especially reds, are prone to fading if subjected to strong sunlight for long periods without the benefit of polish protection. Sometimes proprietary paint restorers and/or paint cutting/rubbing compounds will retrieve the situation. Often a respray is the only real solution.

Dimples

Dimples in the paintwork are caused by the residue of polish (particularly silicone types) not being removed properly before respraying. Paint removal and repainting is the only solution.

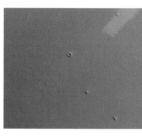

Dents

Small dents are usually easily cured by the 'Dentmaster', or equivalent process, which sucks or pushes out the dent (as long as the paint surface is still intact). Companies offering dent removal services usually come to your home; consult your telephone directory or the internet.

15 Problems due to lack of use

– just like their owners, MINIs need exercise!

Oil

Check the colour and consistency of the engine oil on the dipstick. If golden and not gritty all should be well, if dark and black then the oil will need replacing.

Brakes

If the car you're looking at has been sitting for a while, expect some light rust on the discs. However, this should wear off quickly once the car is used. If the corrosion is more severe, new discs, probably pads too, will be needed.

Tyres

These have a finite life, being at their best for around five years, after which they'll start to harden and deteriorate. If the car you're looking at has been unused, with under-inflated tyres, there's a good chance that the tyres will have flat spots.

Rubber components

Rubber will degrade over time, so pay particular attention to the hoses and seals.

Air-conditioning

Any air-conditioning system needs to be run regularly, if not it will not work efficiently.

Paintwork

As MINI paintwork is soft, any bird droppings on the bodywork (often found on cars not used regularly) should be removed quickly, as they can cause damage.

MINI paint is soft; any bird droppings should be removed quickly or the finish will be damaged.

If air-conditioning is fitted, make sure it's working correctly.

16 The Community

– key people, organisations and companies in the MINI world

As more MINIs have found owners, clubs have been formed around the world. Originally formed in 2001, website MINI2.com provided a forum to support owners worldwide, as well as club meets, product reviews and first drive features of New MINI models. Many owners and enthusiasts have now moved over to totalmini. com, which has the same features, including an active forum and social activities. US owners are well supported by the motoringfile.com website. No club is directly affiliated with MINI, but many, such as the BMW Car Club, have close ties.

The huge amount of engine and bodywork modifications available are, for many, the key attraction to ownership and, with a JCW Cooper S pushing out over 200bhp as an example, it's obvious why such modifications have appeal. Then there are the styling options, and with virtually limitless parts available customising your car can become addictive. Either way, clubs/forums are a great way to see what modifications are hot on the MINI scene and what's good to buy.

In addition to the websites and clubs, there are magazines devoted to the MINI, in particular MC2 (USA) and Modern MINI (UK).

Motorsport

The BMW MINI is proven on the track, with the Cooper making its debut in the John Cooper Challenge in 2002. Created by Mike Cooper in memory of his father, it's a multi-discipline race series recognised by the RAC Motor Sports Association (MSA). Changes from 2004 saw a class for the Cooper S added, and from 2006, with BMW acquiring the name, race preparation was managed by the MINI Motorsport Centre. Cooper and Cooper S cars still participate in one class alongside later R56 models, as part of the renamed MINI Challenge series. Heavily modified Cooper S models also participate in the Time Attack series.

Specialists

As MINI is part of the BMW Group, the dealer network has good coverage in most countries. A MINI dealer will know the car best, offer high standards of service and have the best access to parts. As owners of older MINIs may question using the main dealer for servicing and repairs, a number of independent specialists have sprung up. They also offer a range of aftermarket modifications. Only official dealers will offer JCW parts which are officially recognised by MINI, but if you're after something more extreme, independents will have the best variety of mods and accessories. However, make sure that your chosen MINI specialist's staff are trained to BMW standards. Owners' forums are a good place for recommendations.

Websites

MINI ww.mini.co.uk
MINI Challenge www.minichallenge.co.uk
Total MINI owners' forum www.totalmini.com
MINI2 owners' forum www.mini2.com
National Mini Owners' club www.miniownersclub.co.uk
Motoringfile www.motoringfile.com

Mini Cooper Register www.minicooper.org
BMW Club MINI register www.bmwcarclubgb.co.uk
North American Motoring www.northamericanmotoring.com
MINI Owners' club Malaysia www.miniclubmalaysia.com
Mini Club of Ireland www.miniclub.ie
MINI Torque www.minitorque.com

Books

New MINI, by Graham Robson, Haynes Publishing. ISBN: 978-1840466409
New MINI Performance Manual, by Tim Mundy, Haynes Publishing. ISBN: 978-1844251223
You & Your New MINI, Buying, Enjoying, Maintaining, Modifying, by Tim Mundy, Haynes Publishing. ISBN: 978-1844250288

17 Vital statistics
– essential data at your fingertips

Model	Engine size (cc)	bhp	Top speed (mph)	0-62mph (secs)	Price ●x	Year
One	1598	90	112	10.9	10,300	2001
One D	1364	75	103	13.5	12,220	2003
One D (face-lift)	1364	88	109	11.9	12,225	2005
Cooper	1598	115	124	9.2	11,600	2001
Cooper JCW	1598	132	127	8.5	14,100	2001
Cooper S	1598	163	135	7.4	14,500	2002
Cooper S (face-lift)	1598	170	138	7.2	15,180	2005
Cooper S JCW	1598	200	140	6.8	18,074	2003
Cooper S JCW (face-lift)	1598	210	143	6.6	18,780	2005
Cooper S JCW GP Kit	1598	215	149	6.5	22,000	2006
Cooper (R56)	1598	118	126	9.1	12,995	2006
Cooper S (R56)	1598	173	140	7.1	15,995	2006

The following specifications are for base first or second generation MINI Cooper S versions.

Engine
MINI Cooper S 2002-2006
Type: 1598cc four-cylinder, mounted transversely, aluminium head alloy block Roots supercharger with air-cooled intercooler
Bore/stroke: 77.9/85.8mm
Compression ratio: 8.3:1

Valves: Four valves per cylinder, single overhead camshaft
Ignition: electronic
Induction: multi-point fuel-injection
Power output: 163bhp at 6000rpm
Torque: 155lb ft at 4000rpm

MINI Cooper S 2006
Type: 1598cc four-cylinder, mounted transversely, aluminium head and block, twin-scroll turbocharger
Bore/stroke: 77.0/85.8mm
Compression ratio: 10.5:1

Valves: Four valves per cylinder, single overhead camshaft
Ignition: electronic
Induction: direct fuel-injection
Power output: 173bhp at 5500rpm
Torque: 177lb ft between 1600-5000rpm

Transmission
MINI Cooper S 2002-2006
Front-wheel drive
Gearbox: six-gear manual
Gear ratios mph per 1000rpm: 1st 4.17/6.3, 2nd 2.62/10.1, 3rd 1.33/13.5, 4th 1.09/16.5, 5th 1.33/19.8, 6th 1.09/24.3 final drive: 2.74 (1st, 2nd, 5th, 6th) 4.05 (3rd, 4th)

MINI Cooper S 2006
Front-wheel drive
Gearbox: six-gear manual
Gear ratios mph per 1000rpm: 1st 3.308/6.0, 2nd 2.13/94, 3rd 1.483/13.4, 4th 1.139/17.5, 5th 0.949/21.0, 6th 0.816/24.4 final drive: 3.647

Suspension and steering
MINI Cooper S 2002-2006
Suspension (front): MacPherson struts, coil springs, anti-roll bar; **(rear):** Z-axle, longitudinal struts, coil springs, anti-roll bar
Steering: rack-and-pinion, electric power-assistance, lock-to-lock 2.5 turns
Turning circle: 10.7m

MINI Cooper S 2006
Suspension (front): MacPherson struts, coil springs, anti-roll bar; **(rear):** Z-axle, longitudinal struts, coil springs, anti-roll bar
Steering: rack-and-pinion, electric power-assistance, lock-to-lock 2.4 turns
Turning circle: 10.5m

Brakes
MINI Cooper S 2002-2006
ABS system **Front:** 276mm ventilated discs, **Rear:** 259mm solid discs

MINI Cooper S 2006
ABS system **Front:** 294mm ventilated discs; **Rear:** 259mm solid discs

Dimensions
MINI Cooper S 2002-2006
Length: 3655mm, Width: 1925mm, Height: 1401mm
Wheelbase: 2467mm
Luggage capacity: 150 litres
Front track: 1460mm, **Rear track:** 1466mm
Wheels: 6.5Jx16in alloy

MINI Cooper S 2006
Length: 3714mm, Width: 1683mm, Height: 1407mm
Wheelbase: 2467mm
Luggage capacity: 160 litres
Front track: 1453mm, **Rear track:** 1461mm
Wheels: 6.5Jx16in alloy

Electrical
Battery: 12V 52Ah (R53); 12V 70Ah (R56)
Alternator: 12V 105A (R53); 12V 120A (R56)

Chassis numbers
The 17-digit vehicle identification number (VIN) can be found on the right-hand side front chassis leg in the engine bay. The VIN is also marked in the right-hand corner of the front windscreen.

 **CITROËN 2CV**
978-1-845840-99-0

 MORRIS MINOR & 1000
978-1-845841-01-0

 MERCEDES-BENZ 280-560SL & SLC
978-1-845841-07-2

 MERCEDES-BENZ PAGODA 230, 250 & 280SL
978-1-845841-13-3

 JAGUAR/DAIMLER XJ6, XJ12 & Sovereign
978-1-845841-19-5

 **ROLLS-ROYCE SILVER SHADOW & BENTLEY T-SERIES**
978-1-845841-46-1

 FIAT 500 & 600
978-1-845841-47-8

 JAGUAR XJ-S
978-1-845841-61-4

 SUBARU IMPREZA
978-1-845841-63-8

 BSA Bantam
978-1-845841-65-2

 Ford CAPRI
978-1-845842-05-5

 MX-5 MIATA
978-1-845842-31-4

 Triumph STAG
978-1-845842-70-3

 Norton Commando
978-1-845842-81-9

 Peugeot 205 GTI
978-1-845842-83-3

 HONDA CBR FireBlade
978-1-845843-07-6

 HONDA CBR600 HURRICANE
978-1-845843-09-0

 Triumph TR7 & TR8
978-1-845843-16-8

 CORVETTE C2
978-1-845843-29-8

 Porsche 911SC
978-1-845843-30-4

 LAND ROVER SERIES I, II & IIA
978-1-845843-48-9

 MG TD, TF & TF1500
978-1-845843-52-6

 Austin SEVEN
978-1-845843-53-3

 MG & AUSTIN-HEALEY MIDGET & SPRITE
978-1-845843-54-0

 Triumph Spitfire & GT6
978-1-845843-56-4

 JAGUAR XK 120, 140 & 150
978-1-845843-77-9

 MG MGA
978-1-845843-91-5

 BIG HEALEYS
978-1-845843-92-2

 Triumph Herald & Vitesse
978-1-845843-93-9

 Cobra replicas
978-1-845843-95-3

Porsche 986 BOXSTER
978-1-845844-23-3

Porsche 987 BOXSTER & CAYMAN
978-1-845844-24-0

Jaguar XJ6, XJ8 & XJR
978-1-845844-34-9

Land Rover Series III
978-1-845844-42-4

BMW E30 3 SERIES
978-1-845844-43-1

ALFA ROMEO GIULIA GT COUPÉ
978-1-904788-69-0

PORSCHE 928
978-1-904788-70-6

VOLKSWAGEN BEETLE
978-1-904788-72-0

JAGUAR E-type
978-1-904788-85-0

ALFA ROMEO GIULIA SPIDER
978-1-904788-98-0

More from Veloce –

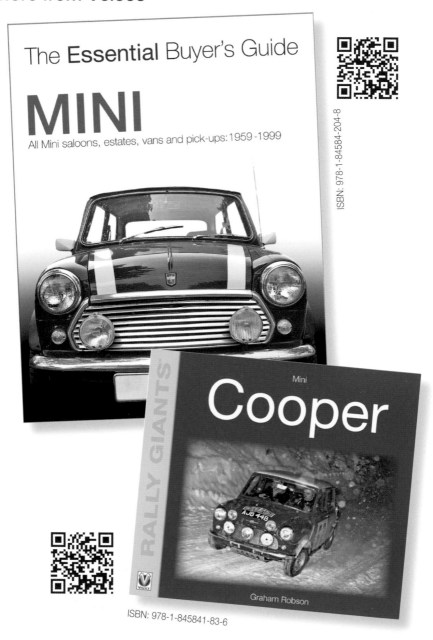

The **Essential** Buyer's Guide

MINI

All Mini saloons, estates, vans and pick-ups: 1959-1999

ISBN: 978-1-84584-204-8

RALLY GIANTS

Mini

Cooper

Graham Robson

ISBN: 978-1-845841-83-6

For more information visit us at www.veloce.co.uk or

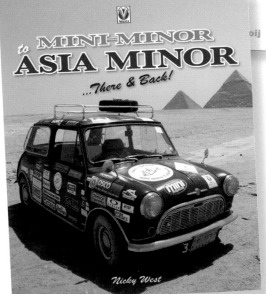

Index